THIS BOOK BELONGS TO:

Lillian

Doodle Devotions for Kids

Copyright © 2019 by Christian Art Kids, an imprint of Christian Art Publishers, PO Box 1599, Vereeniging, 1930, RSA

© 2019
First edition 2019

Designed by Christian Art Kids

Images used under license from Shutterstock.com

Scripture quotations are taken from the Holy Bible, New Living Translation®, copyright © 1996, 2004, 2007, 2013, 2015 by Tyndale House Foundation. Used by permission of Tyndale House Publishers, Inc., Carol Stream, Illinois 60188. All rights reserved.

Printed in China

ISBN 978-1-4321-2712-1

19   20   21   22   23   24   25   26   27   28   –   11   10   9   8   7   6   5   4   3   2

Printed in Shenzhen, China
November 2019
Print Run: 100647

DOODLE Devotions FOR KIDS

christian art kids

~ NANCY TAYLOR ~

Contents

The Old Testament

The New Testament

THE OLD TESTAMENT

Creation

READ: Genesis 1:1–2:3

THINK

God created a beautiful, perfect world out of nothing. First there was complete emptiness, and then six days later there was a whole world of amazingness. First God made light and dark, day and night, sea and dry land. It was a very beautiful world. Then He filled the earth with wonderful plants for us to enjoy and eat from, and amazing and funny animals. Isn't it incredible to think that God created everything we can see and taste and touch and smell out of nothing?

When He had the whole garden ready, God made people to live in it and take care of it, a man and a woman named Adam and Eve. The Bible tells us that God made them in His image, which means that every human on earth reflects a little bit of what God is like. Adam and Eve really had it made, with all those plants to eat and animals to name. And since sin hadn't yet entered the world, everything was perfect. No weeds or sickness or death. No mosquitoes. No bad days. It was all very good. What a wonderful God, and what a wonderful world!

DRAW:

What's your favorite part of creation? Is there a plant you think is beautiful or an animal that you think is really cool? On the next page, draw a garden with all your favorite plants and animals in it. Think about our powerful creator God who made everything, and praise Him for the wonderful world He made for us to enjoy.

"God created human beings in his own image."

Genesis 1:27

One Rule

READ: Genesis 2:15-17

THINK

Adam and Eve were given an amazing garden to live in and care for. It was beautiful and life was easy. God only gave them one rule: Don't eat from one particular tree in the middle of the garden, the tree of the knowledge of good and evil. He warned them that if they disobeyed this one rule and ate fruit from that tree, they would die. I bet it seemed like a pretty simple rule at first. They could have anything they wanted except the fruit from one tree.

But every day they passed that tree, Adam and Eve kept thinking about how great that fruit looked. They probably wondered if what God told them was really true. How could such beautiful fruit kill them? Surely one bite couldn't be that big of a deal. We call that feeling of wanting something we know we aren't supposed to have *temptation*. When we are tempted to do something wrong, we have to choose whether we will fight against the temptation and do what is right, or give in to it and do what is wrong.

DRAW:

Rules are like that—we don't want something until we've been told we can't have it. And then suddenly it's all we can think about. Think of some of the rules you have to obey. On the next page, write out some of the rules that are hard for you to obey. Ask God to help you obey them.

.--------------------------------

The Lord God warned him, "You may freely eat
the fruit of every tree in the garden— except
the tree of the knowledge of good and evil.
If you eat its fruit, you are sure to die."

Genesis 2:16-17

A Big Problem

READ: Genesis 3:1-7

THINK

Life in the Garden of Eden was great, until one day Satan, disguised as a snake, came and tempted Eve to eat fruit from the tree God had commanded them not to eat from. He told lies that made her doubt God's word and God's goodness, and she ate the fruit. Adam ate some too. And in that instant sin entered the world. Things would never be the same again. The first thing that happened is Adam and Eve noticed they were naked, and they were ashamed. That was a new feeling for them. Then they realized that they kept on wanting to do wrong things. We are like that too. Because of that first sin, every person is born a sinner and continues to fight against God throughout their whole life. All of us do wrong things every day.

The good news is that Jesus came to take away our sins. We can be forgiven because He took the punishment for our sin when He died on the cross. But we're getting ahead of ourselves. It would be a long time before Jesus would be born in Bethlehem and then die on the cross. . .

DRAW:

Think of some wrong things you've done, even today. Write or doodle them on the next page. Now take a thick black marker and cross those sins out. When we tell Jesus we're sorry for the wrong things we do, He forgives us and takes those bad things away and makes it as if we had never even done them.

The woman was convinced. She saw that the tree was beautiful and its fruit looked delicious, and she wanted the wisdom it would give her. So she took some of the fruit and ate it. Then she gave some to her husband, who was with her, and he ate it, too.

Genesis 3:6

A Bigger Promise

READ: Genesis 3:8-24

THINK:

On the day Adam and Eve disobeyed God, when God came for His evening walk with them, they hid. They were so ashamed of what they had done that they didn't want to see Him or be with Him. That's what sin does—it separates us from God and from other people and makes us want to hide. But of course it's impossible to hide from God, since He's everywhere. Even when we are so ashamed of our sin that we try to run from God, He comes and finds us because He wants to have a relationship with us.

God listened to Adam and Eve blame each other, trying to push responsibility for their sin onto someone else. And then He gave them some bad news. Their actions had brought pain and evil into the world. The plants and animals would now fight against them, and they couldn't even stay in the garden anymore. Life would be filled with pain and struggle and sickness because their sin had changed everything. But there was a little bit of good news, too. God promised that one day there would be a person who would crush Satan. And that person was Jesus! He came to break the power that sin has over our hearts and over the world.

DRAW: Draw a picture of a garden, and imagine yourself walking with God in the garden just like Adam and Eve did. God wants to be with you so much that He sent Jesus to make a way for you to be friends with Him.

When the cool evening breezes
were blowing, the man and
his wife heard the Lord God walking
about in the garden. So they hid from
the Lord God among the trees.

Genesis 3:8

A Big Flood

READ: Genesis 6-8

THINK

Just a short time after Adam and Eve, the world had become so evil that God was sorry He had even created it. Sin had messed everything up so badly that it was almost beyond hope. But with God, nothing is hopeless.

There was still one person who walked with God, a man named Noah. God told him to build a very big boat, called an ark. There was no rain yet, so building a big boat seemed like a silly idea, but Noah believed God and obeyed. When it was done, God filled the ark with two of every kind of animal and told Noah and his family to get on board. When everyone was safely inside, God shut the door—and then the rain started. It rained for forty days and forty nights, and everything on earth was wiped out in a huge flood except for Noah and his family and the animals on the boat. God kept them safe, and when the storm was over He placed a rainbow in the sky and promised He would never again destroy the whole earth with a flood.

Imagine what would have happened if Noah hadn't obeyed God. We need to be like Noah and obey God even if it doesn't make sense and even if people make fun of us for it. When we trust in God's Word, we are safe forever.

DRAW:

The story of Noah's ark is a great reminder of God's power to save. If He could use one man to build a boat one-and-a-half football fields long and five stories high, and then keep him safe inside that boat when everything else on earth was destroyed, we can trust that God can save us, too. On the next page, draw Noah, his family, and the animals in the boat, and color in the rainbow that reminds us of God's promise to protect the earth.

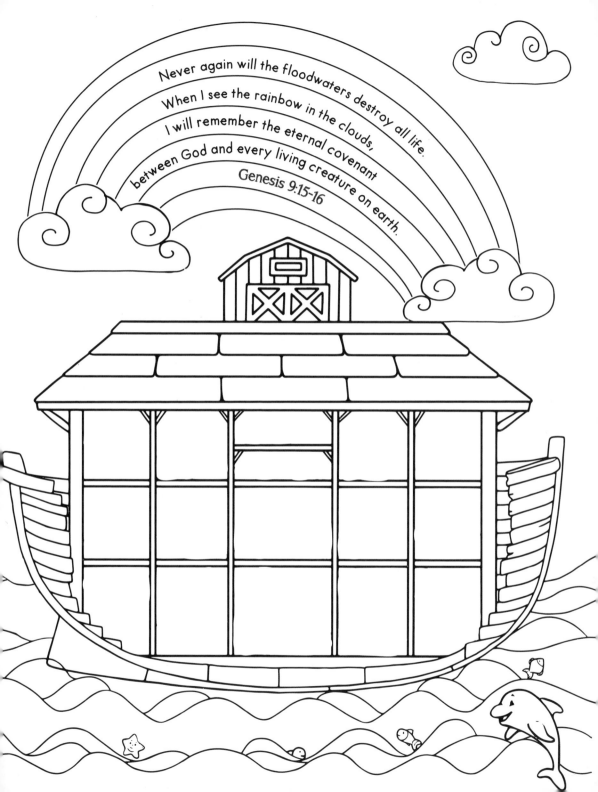

Never again will the floodwaters destroy all life.
When I see the rainbow in the clouds,
I will remember the eternal covenant
between God and every living creature on earth.
Genesis 9:15-16

Another Promise

THINK

Remember how God made a promise to Adam and Eve that He would send a deliverer to save them from the curse of sin? God hadn't forgotten. A few hundred years later He appeared to a man named Abraham, and He told him that his wife would have a son, and that son would have sons, and when everything was said and done his descendants would be as numerous as the stars. Not only that, but the entire world would be blessed through him. What God was really promising is that one of his descendants would be the promised one, the Son of God, who would pay the price for our sin so we could live with Him forever.

There was just one problem: Abraham and his wife, Sarah, were too old to have a baby. It was an impossible promise. But do you know what? Abraham believed God anyway, and God kept His promise! What is impossible for us is no big deal to God. Abraham and Sarah had Isaac, and many, many generations later one of his descendants, Mary, had Jesus. All the nations of the world were blessed through Him because now anyone who believes in Him, like Abraham did, will be saved forever.

DRAW:

The baby Isaac was a wonderful gift to Abraham and Sarah, but the even better gift was that because Abraham believed in God's promise, he was saved. And we can be saved, too, if we believe that Jesus died for our sins. On the next page, color in the word *believe* and think about God's promises that you believe in.

Because of Abraham's faith,
God counted him as righteous. . . .
God will also count us as righteous if
we believe in him, the one who raised Jesus
our Lord from the dead. He was handed over
to die because of our sins, and he was raised
to life to make us right with God.

Romans 4:22, 24-25

Brothers & Enemies

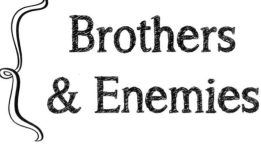

THINK

Isaac grew up to have twin boys—Jacob and Esau. Like many siblings, the two brothers did not get along. For one thing, they didn't have much in common. Esau was a hunter who liked adventure; Jacob liked to stay home by himself. On top of that, Jacob was jealous of Esau. He even managed to trick Esau into trading his inheritance—the money and blessing he would get as the oldest son when their father died—for a bowl of soup!

When Isaac was about to die, he called Esau in and told him to go hunting, cook the meat from the animal he killed, and then bring it back so he could give him a blessing. Jacob's mother, Rebekah, overheard his instructions and came up with a plan for Jacob to get the blessing instead: she would cook some meat from their herd of animals and dress Jacob up to fool Isaac into thinking he was Esau. The plan worked like a charm, and Jacob got the blessing. But Esau was pretty angry about his little brother stealing his blessing, and Jacob had to run away and live with his uncle because he was afraid Esau would kill him. Both brothers missed out on the joy of living together and enjoying each other because of their rivalry.

DRAW:

Are you ever jealous of your brothers and sisters? Do you try to steal the attention from your parents? Learn from Jacob and Esau, and don't let arguments divide you. On the next page, draw a picture of your brothers and sisters, and think of some things you can do to show them how much you love them.

Keep on loving each other as brothers and sisters.

Hebrews 13:1

God Meant It for Good

READ: Genesis 50:14-24

THINK

The full story about Joseph, Jacob's youngest son, takes up fourteen chapters in the Bible (Genesis 37–50), so let me give you the short version. Jacob loved Joseph more than his other 11 sons, and that made his brothers (understandably) jealous. So one day they decided to sell Joseph into slavery and tell their father that he had been killed by wild animals. Not very nice of them, huh? But God was with Joseph, and He gave him a special ability to tell the king what his dreams meant. One of his dreams predicted that there would be seven years of bumper crops, followed by seven years of famine. Sure enough, the dream came true. Because they knew ahead of time what would happen, Joseph was able to save enough grain from the seven years of plenty to see them through the seven years of famine.

Back home, Joseph's family didn't have enough to eat because of the famine, but they heard that there was grain in Egypt, so they went there, and they ended up standing before Joseph and asking for food. They didn't recognize Joseph, but he recognized them. You would think he might be angry with them. But rather than trying to pay them back for what they had done to him, Joseph said, "You meant it for evil, but God meant it for good." Their evil act of selling their brother to be a slave was the very thing God used to save people from starving during the famine.

DRAW:

Sometimes the bad things that happen are the very things God uses to help us learn to trust Him more or even enable us to help other people. Draw some of the hard things in your life that God has used for good. Maybe a friend was unkind to you, but it enabled you to make a new friend. Or maybe you broke your leg but that meant you were able to spend more time with your family.

You intended to harm me, but God intended it all for good. He brought me to this position so I could save the lives of many people.

Genesis 50:20

A Baby in a Basket

READ: Exodus 2:1-10

The famine brought Jacob and his sons to Egypt, and there they became a great nation, as God had promised. But eventually God's people, the Israelites as they were called, became slaves in Egypt. Life was very hard for them. In fact, King Pharaoh commanded that all the baby boys born to Israelite women should be killed. But a few of the nurse-midwives feared God more than they feared the Pharaoh, so they let the boys live.

One of those boys was so beautiful and precious that his parents kept him hidden for a few months. They just couldn't bear to let him die. When it became too dangerous to keep him hidden—babies are pretty noisy, after all—his mother put him in a basket, coated it with tar to make it float, and put it in the river. As the baby's sister watched, who should come upon the baby in the basket but the daughter of Pharaoh? She loved the sweet baby, and so she decided to adopt him. She called him Moses, which means "to draw out," because she had drawn him out of the water.

As all this was happening, Moses' sister came out and said that her mother would be happy to take care of the baby until he was old enough to live with the princess, and she agreed. God had miraculously saved this little baby from being killed and made a way for his own mother to take care of him.

 DRAW:

Moses' story shows how God can work in seemingly impossible situations. Has God done something miraculous in your life? It may not be a big thing, but God is at work every day to put us in just the right situations to help us grow and use us to help others. Draw a picture of one way you've seen God at work in your life.

It was by faith that Moses' parents hid him for three months when he was born. They saw that God had given them an unusual child, and they were not afraid to disobey the king's command.

Hebrews 11:23

A Burning Call

READ: Exodus 3:1-4:17

THINK

There he was, minding his own business, keeping track of his father-in-law's sheep, when suddenly Moses saw a bush on fire. That might have caught his attention, but he certainly couldn't ignore it when he noticed that the bush didn't burn up! Moses went over to see what was going on, and then God spoke to him, telling him that the ground he was standing on was holy. That would be scary enough, but next God said that He had heard the cries of His people and would use Moses to save them.

Who, me? Moses wasn't sure he was up to the task. The land God was promising to bring them to sounded great, but he was pretty sure God had chosen the wrong guy to lead the march. He wasn't a good public speaker, and he really didn't even want to lead anybody anywhere, let alone an entire nation through the wilderness. But God didn't back down. He knew that Moses was the right person for the job because He was going to be with him every step of the way. It wasn't up to Moses, it was up to God. And God can do anything!

DRAW:

Color in the flames on the burning bush, and the green leaves. Imagine what it would be like to hear God speak. What things has God asked you to do? Write those things in the space around the bush.

"Now go! I will be with you as you speak, and I will instruct you in what to say. "

Exodus 4:12

Frogs, Flies, Fleas, & Other Creepy-Crawlies

THINK

READ: Exodus 7:14–12:32

❁ God had told Moses that He would free His people from slavery in Egypt, and He did just that. But it took a while. Pharaoh did not want his free labor to disappear into the wilderness, and he was very stubborn. Over and over again Moses and his brother, Aaron, told Pharaoh that God wanted him to let the Hebrew people go. Each time Pharaoh refused, and each time God showed him who was boss. First the Nile River turned to blood and all the fish died. Then there were frogs covering the land— even in people's cooking bowls and beds! Next there were gnats and flies. Then the livestock all got sick and died. Next everybody's skin broke out in boils. Then hail damaged all the crops. Locusts came and ate everything that was left. Then there was darkness over the whole land for three days. Still Pharaoh would not obey God and let His people go.

Finally God sent the worst plague of all. The oldest boy of every household in Egypt would die except for the people who killed a lamb and wiped its blood on their doorpost. You see, God was sending a sign: He would save His people with the blood of a lamb. For now it was a literal lamb, but one day it would be the Lamb of God, Jesus, who would die to save His people.

DRAW:

When the people killed a baby lamb and wiped its blood on their doorposts, they were saying that they believed God and trusted Him alone to save them. And that's how we are saved, too — by the blood Jesus shed on the cross in our place. In the space on the next page, color in the cross and write a prayer thanking Jesus for being the Lamb of God who took away the sin of the whole world.

"Look! The Lamb of God who takes
away the sin of the world!"

John 1:29

Red Sea Rescue

READ: Exodus 13:17–14:31

THINK

Finally Pharaoh had let God's people go. God had kept His promise, and everything was looking pretty good. But then Pharaoh remembered how great his free labor had been, and he regretted letting them go. He gathered up his army and chased the Israelites into the wilderness. There were God's people, with a big ocean called the Red Sea on one side and the Egyptian army on the other. Things were suddenly looking not-so-great. Had God left them? No, of course not!

Moses told the people, "Don't be afraid. Stand firm, and see the salvation of the Lord." And then he raised up his staff and stretched his arm over the sea, and the water divided. Some of it piled up on the right, and some of it piled up on the left, and in between was dry ground that the people could walk across. It was a powerful miracle! Even the Egyptians saw that God was powerful to save His people, and they were afraid of Him. But they didn't act quite fast enough, and the water came over them and they were swept into the sea.

 DRAW:

The crossing of the Red Sea was a very big moment in the history of God's people. Even now sometimes people talk about a Red-Sea moment, meaning a time when they are trapped with no way out except if God decides to save them. And God always does save. Maybe not in the way we want, and maybe not in this life, but He does save us for all eternity if we put our trust in Him. On the next page, draw the people walking through the Red Sea, and remember that God is powerful to save us even when things look impossible.

But Moses told the people, "Don't be afraid. Just stand still and watch the LORD rescue you today. The Egyptians you see today will never be seen again."

Exodus 14:13

Bread from Heaven

READ: Exodus 16

THINK

Experts think there were about 2.4 million Israelites who left Egypt. That's a lot of people for one leader (Moses) to lead and feed. There they were, on the far side of the Red Sea, camped beside a spring. There was no city, no 24-hour grocery store, just a whole lot of wilderness. What would they eat? The people started grumbling, and even began to wonder if they were better off back in Egypt, living as slaves. Fortunately, our God is a big God, and nothing is too hard for Him.

God could have brought His people to an area with enough grain and fruit to feed them. But He wanted them to learn to trust Him, so instead He fed them directly from His own hand. He sent bread straight from heaven each night. It was called *manna*, which means, "what is it?" No one could doubt that it was God who provided for them each day. And God provides for us each day, too. In fact, not only does God provide food and shelter for us, He gives us something better—Himself! Jesus said "I am the bread of life" (John 6:35). He gave Himself as a sacrifice to save us from sin and death, and if we believe in Him and find our joy in Him, we will be fully satisfied forever.

DRAW:

Each day God gives us many wonderful gifts,
but sometimes we forget to notice them. What has God
provided for you today? Draw some of God's gifts to you,
and thank Him for providing them!

He rained down manna for them to eat; he gave them bread
from heaven. They ate the food of angels! God gave
them all they could hold.

Psalm 78:24-25

Words to Live By

READ: Exodus 20:1-21

THINK

God's people had just escaped from slavery in Egypt. They had a leader, Moses, but they didn't have any laws to govern how they should live. God knew that they needed rules to teach them right and wrong so that they could live in peace with one another. And so He called Moses up on the mountain and gave him ten commandments. If the people obeyed these laws of God, things would go well for them. They would not need to be afraid of each other and they would know that they were pleasing God.

The ten commandments are the basics of how to please God, and they apply to us today as well. The first four laws teach us to fear God more than people: Give God first place in your heart, don't think of anything as more important than Him, honor His name, and set aside one day a week to worship Him and rest. The next six laws teach us how to live with other people: honor your parents, do not kill, be faithful to your husband or wife, do not steal, do not lie, and do not be jealous. If you obey these commandments, you will be living God's way.

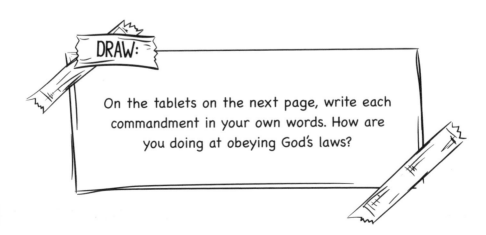

DRAW:

On the tablets on the next page, write each commandment in your own words. How are you doing at obeying God's laws?

"I am the LORD your God, who rescued you from the land of Egypt, the place of your slavery. You must not have any other god but me."

Exodus 20:2-3

1. ----------------------------------
   ----

2. ----------------------------------
   ----

3. ----------------------------------
   ----

4. ----------------------------------
   ----

5. ----------------------------------
   ----

6. ----------------------------------
   ----

7. ----------------------------------
   ----

8. ----------------------------------
   ----

9. ----------------------------------
   ----

10. ----------------------------------

The Tabernacle

READ: Exodus 26

THINK

Once the Israelites were established as a nation, God gave very specific instructions for making a huge tent, called the Tabernacle. It was the house where God would live with His people. Because God is holy, it had to be a very special house made exactly His way. Because He wanted to live among His people and have a relationship with them, it had to be in a portable tent until they could settle in the land God had promised them.

The Tabernacle shows us that God is holy and separate—there was a special room in the Tabernacle called the Most Holy Place where God lived, and even the priests weren't allowed to go in there more than once a year. But it also shows us how much God wants to be with us. He was willing to go through the wilderness with His people, even though they repeatedly rejected Him, disobeyed Him, and worshiped idols.

When Jesus came, He was called Emmanuel—God with us—and the Bible says He "tabernacled" among us. He became a human, lived a sinless life, and then died in our place so that we can be with Him forever. When Jesus returned to heaven, He left the Holy Spirit to be His presence on earth. Now, instead of having to go to a particular building to meet with God, we can talk to Him anytime, anywhere.

DRAW:

On the next page, draw some of the places where you like to go to be with God. Is it your room? A particular chair that is warm and cozy? A special place outside?

So the Word became human
and made his home among us. He
was full of unfailing love and
faithfulness. And we have seen
his glory, the glory of the
Father's one and only Son.

John 1:14

12 Spies

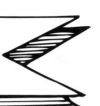

THINK

📖 **READ: Numbers 13**

🎈 I don't know about you, but I love a really great spy story. And the Bible has several! God's people were standing on the edge of the land God had promised to give them. But first they needed to see what they were up against. So they sent 12 men to spy out the land. The only problem was that what they saw was pretty scary. The land was as wonderful as God had said it would be—flowing with milk and honey. But the people who lived there were strong and their cities were well-protected. In their own strength, God's people didn't stand a chance. And so, on the negative report of 10 of the 12 spies, the people chickened out. They were so scared that they even begged Moses to take them back to Egypt!

What the spies were really saying is that they didn't trust God. He had promised them the land, and He is way more powerful than any giant or army. God would be faithful to help them conquer the land He was calling them to. But they refused to trust Him, and so they were forced to wander in the wilderness for 40 years before they were allowed to conquer the Promised Land.

DRAW:

What kinds of things are you afraid of? Everyone is scared sometimes, but God is faithful. He will always be with us and will help us when we ask Him to. On the next page, draw some things you're afraid of, and ask God to help you to trust Him even in those scary things.

WHEN
I AM afRaid,
I will PUT MY
TRUST IN YOU
Psalm 56:3

Spy Story, Take Two

THINK

READ: Joshua 2

Today's story is another great spy story. It was now 40 years later, and God's people once again stood on the edge of the land God had promised to give them. Joshua, one of the original 12 spies, was now the leader of the whole nation, and he sent two spies to scout out the city of Jericho. Someone told the king of Jericho about the spies, and so he hunted them down. The Israelite spies only escaped because a woman named Rahab hid them on the roof of her house under some grain. When the king's men came hunting for them, she told them the Israelites had fled into the wilderness. Now, Rahab had done a lot of bad things in her life, but this time she made a choice to stand for God and protect His people. And God saved her and her family because of her faith. In fact, one of her descendants was Jesus!

Have you done some things that you know were wrong? We all have—the Bible tells us that every single person is a sinner, and none of us can save ourselves. But any of us can be saved, just like Rahab was. Nothing you can ever do will make God love you less, and He is standing with open arms to welcome you back the moment you tell Him you're sorry for your sin.

DRAW:

As you color the verse on the next page, think about some of the things you've done wrong and tell God you're sorry. He will always forgive you the moment you repent.

Those Tumblin' Down Walls

READ: Joshua 6

THINK

☙ The city of Jericho was barricaded shut because the people who lived there were afraid of the Israelites. It was a mighty and well-fortified city, with a wall 6 feet (2 meters) thick and 26 feet (8 meters) high. God had promised to give the Israelites victory over the city, but He was going to do it His way. And His way made the people look a little silly. Instead of attacking the city, God told them to march around it, once a day for six days and then seven times on the seventh day. No battering rams or flaming arrows or war cries—just silent marching. I would guess that some of God's people had their doubts about this plan, but they had learned by this point to trust that God knew what He was doing, so they obeyed. And God kept His promise. That huge thick wall fell down flat the second they finished marching around the final time!

Do you trust God that much? Will you obey Him even when His laws seem silly? Even when it's easier to tell a little lie? Or to go along with your friends even though you know you shouldn't? God's ways are always best, even when doing things our way seems simpler.

DRAW:

On the next page, draw a picture of the people marching around the wall of Jericho. As you draw, think about how you can trust God and obey Him even when it seems easier to do things your own way.

When the people heard the sound of the rams' horns, they shouted as loud as they could. Suddenly, the walls of Jericho collapsed, and the Israelites charged straight into the town and captured it.

Joshua 6:20

God Calling

READ: 1 Samuel 3

THINK

❦ We're going to skip forward a few hundred years in Israel's history. They were now living in the land God had promised them, but they failed to obey God and conquer it completely, and as a result there were a lot of problems. The people had almost forgotten God because they started worshiping the idols of the pagan people who lived in the land with them. But God still had His hand on Israel, and there were some people who remained faithful to Him. One of those people was a woman named Hannah. She desperately wanted a baby, and so she begged God to give her a son—and He did. The baby was named Samuel, and when he was old enough, his mother Hannah gave him back to the Lord. He lived in the Tabernacle and served God there.

One night Samuel heard a voice calling him. First he thought it was the old priest, Eli, but finally the fourth time he heard the voice he answered, "Speak, your servant is listening!" And God spoke, telling him what was going to happen to Eli and the nation. God still speaks to us today, primarily through the Bible. We can respond just like Samuel, telling God that we will listen and obey His Word.

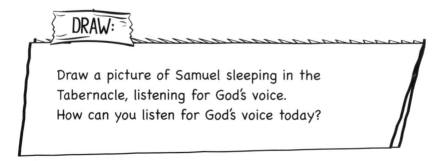

DRAW:

Draw a picture of Samuel sleeping in the
Tabernacle, listening for God's voice.
How can you listen for God's voice today?

And the Lord came and called as before,
"Samuel! Samuel!" And Samuel replied, "Speak, your servant is listening."
1 Samuel 3:10

Who Is Your King?

READ: 1 Samuel 8

THINK

When Samuel grew up, he was an important prophet in Israel. He continued to listen to God and deliver His messages to the people. Unfortunately, Samuel's sons did not follow God, so they couldn't take on his job when he died. The Israelites were worried about who would lead them in the next generation, so they begged Samuel to give them a king. After all, the nations around them all had kings—why shouldn't they?

The problem was, they already had a king—God. In asking for a king, they were not only trying to become like the idol-worshiping nations around them, they were also rejecting God and telling Him that they didn't want to serve Him. This was a very bad idea, and Samuel told them so. If they had a king, he would one day get power hungry and oppress them.

Nevertheless, God told Samuel to go ahead and give the people a king. He gave them over to their own evil desires and let them deal with the consequences of their sinful choice. Sure enough, eventually Israel's kings did oppress the people, just as God had warned them. But God is faithful, and one day many generations later He sent Jesus, the King of kings and Lord of lords, to rescue the people from their sinful choices forever.

DRAW:

We have the same choice the Israelites had—will we let God be our King, or will we reject Him? If we want Him to be our King, we must obey Him. That's the deal. On the next page, color in the crown and think about how you can crown Jesus as King in your heart and in your actions.

GOD IS MY KING

"Do everything they say to you," the LORD replied, "for they are rejecting me, not you. They don't want me to be their king any longer."

1 Samuel 8:7

A Giant Problem

READ: 1 Samuel 17

THINK

God's people had a big problem: the Philistines had decided to fight against them, and they were outnumbered by some over-sized giants. The biggest of them all, a man named Goliath, was over 9 feet tall, and his armor weighed 125 pounds. This giant of a man challenged the Israelites to a one-on-one battle. They could send their best man out to fight him, and the winner would claim the victory for their entire army.

You would think that the Israelites would send out their best and brightest in order to avoid a battle in which they might lose many men, but they were too scared. No one thought they could defeat Goliath—no one except little shepherd boy David, that is. This young man heard Goliath's taunts against the Israelites and their God, and he said, "Let me fight him! I can't beat him on my own, but God can win this battle."

And so little David went out to fight giant Goliath, armed with only a sling and five stones. In his own strength he didn't stand a chance, but with God on his side, he couldn't lose. It didn't even take five stones, either—it took only one. David slung that stone around his head, let it go, and it hit Goliath on the head so that he fell down dead.

DRAW:

When God is on our side, we can win any battle He sends our way. What hard things is God asking you to trust Him to help you with? Draw pictures of those things, and then trust God to help you rely on His strength as you fight those battles.

Everyone assembled here will know that the LORD rescues his people, but not with sword and spear. This is the LORD's battle, and he will give you to us!

1 Samuel 17:47

Doing Things God's Way

READ: 1 Samuel 24

THINK

The first king of Israel, Saul, had turned his back on God and gone insane with his hunger for power and his jealousy against anyone who seemed to be more popular than he was. So God chose David to be the next king. He was a good choice, and the Bible calls him a man after God's own heart. But even though Saul was a terrible king and David was going to be a much better king, God asked David to wait a long time to take the throne. In the meantime, King Saul spent all his time hunting David down and trying to kill him. David had to live in caves and constantly move around so that Saul wouldn't find him.

One day David was in a cave, and who should he come upon but Saul, all alone and totally vulnerable. David could have killed him right then and there. The men who were with him advised him to go ahead and get rid of Saul. Surely this was an opportunity sent straight from God. But David knew God didn't want him to take the throne that way, and so he spared Saul's life. David wanted to do things God's way, in His time, rather than in the way that made the most sense according to the world's wisdom.

DRAW:

What about you? Will you wait and do things God's way, even if there is a shortcut that other people are telling you to take? Do the maze on the following page, and as you do it think about how you can follow God when other people are telling you to do something you know is wrong.

There is a path before each person that seems right, but it ends in death.

Proverbs 14:12

START

FINISH

God's Preparation

THINK

READ: Psalm 23

While David was waiting for God to keep His promise to make him king, he didn't just sit around. For one thing, he wrote a lot of poetry, much of which can be found in the book of Psalms. One of the most famous poems David wrote is Psalm 23, which talks about all the ways God is our good shepherd. He gives us all we need, lets us rest, and guides us on the right path. When we are afraid, He is nearby. When we get hurt, He bandages our wounds. God is faithful and good all the days of our lives, and David's beautiful words remind us of that truth.

David was willing to wait patiently for God to keep His promises, and God used that time to prepare David to be the best possible king for Israel. Your growing-up years are also a time of preparation. The experiences you have, the things you spend your time on, and especially the time you spend learning about God will help you become the person God wants you to be. Are you making the most of your time?

DRAW:

On the next page, draw some of the things
God is using in your life to make you a better
person. It might be good things, like your parents
or your church, or it might be bad things,
like the time you got in trouble and learned
a really important lesson.

Surely your GOODNESS
& UNFAILING LOVE
will pursue me all the days of my life
& I will live in the house of the Lord forever.

Psalm 23:6

David's Big Sin

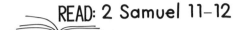 READ: 2 Samuel 11–12

David did finally become king, and for many years he led God's people well. They conquered their enemies and enjoyed a time of peace. He led them in following God. But even the best leaders who really love God can mess up in big ways. One day, when David was home instead of fighting the battle with his men like he should have been, he saw a beautiful woman. He wanted to marry her, but she was someone else's wife. David could have—and definitely should have—left her alone. Sadly, he didn't. He took her as his own, and then when his sin was discovered he had the woman's husband killed in battle. He had disobeyed two of the ten commandments: adultery and murder. And the worst part was, he didn't even realize what he had done.

God sent a prophet named Nathan to point out David's sin, and David was crushed when he came face-to-face with his great sin. He confessed to the Lord, saying, "Against you, and you alone, have I sinned." Then he asked God to cleanse him and create a new heart inside him (Psalm 51:4, 10). And you know what? God did forgive him. There is no sin too great for God to forgive. All we have to do is tell Him what we have done and ask Him to forgive us—and He will!

DRAW:

All of us sin, every day. On the next page, draw or write some of the things you're sorry for, and then ask God to forgive you.

PURIFY ME from my sins, and I will be **CLEAN**; **WASH ME** and I will be whiter than snow. Psalm 51:7

The Gift of Wisdom

THINK

Have you ever read one of those stories about a genie who comes out of a magic lamp and grants 3 wishes? Those are fun stories. What would you ask for if you had that opportunity? There is one man in the Bible who was given the chance to ask for anything he wanted—only the one asking was God Himself, so he was guaranteed that he would get what he asked for. That man was David's son, Solomon, who became the next king after David died. God appeared to him in a dream and said, "What do you want? Ask, and I will give it to you!"

I don't know about you, but in that situation I might be tempted to ask for money or fame. But Solomon didn't ask for anything for himself—he asked for wisdom to lead the people well and know right from wrong. What a great request! And he was asking the right person, because all wisdom comes from God. Solomon's request pleased God so much that He gave him wealth and fame in addition to wisdom. Solomon was the wisest person who ever lived, and he was known throughout the world for his riches.

DRAW:

Okay, your turn. What do you want more than anything else? Draw it on the next page, but remember that the most important things in life are the things we can't see: our relationship with God, our love for others, and our hope for eternal life with Jesus.

WHAT DO YOU WANT?

If you need wisdom, ask our generous God, and he will give it to you. He will not rebuke you for asking. James 1:5

God's House

READ: 2 Chronicles 7

THINK

Do you remember that God had told Moses to make a Tabernacle that would travel with the Israelites from place to place so that God could be with His people? Now, 480 years later, God's people were no longer on the move. They had taken the land God had promised them, and it was time for a more permanent building to house God's presence. And so Solomon built God's Temple, following the instructions that his father, David, had received from God. And what a glorious and beautiful structure it was, all covered in gold. Inside was the most holy place, the place where God dwelt among His people. Around that was a place for sacrifices to be made for the sins of the people. This was the place God commanded the people to come and worship Him.

Many years later Jesus came, and He declared that He Himself is the true Temple (John 1:14, 51; 2:19). He is God who lived among His people. Jesus fulfilled all the requirements of the law, so His death on the cross was the once-for-all final sacrifice. When He died, the curtain separating the Most Holy Place from the rest of the Temple was torn in two from top to bottom. Now we don't need a temple or sacrifices. We can go straight into God's presence at any time through prayer.

DRAW:

Imagine you live in Solomon's time and have to go to the Temple to worship God and make sacrifices for your sins. It would be a lot of work, wouldn't it? But we don't have to do that anymore. Draw a picture of what you feel like when you go into God's presence through prayer, or of the place where you feel closest to Him.

And so, dear brothers and sisters, we can boldly enter heaven's Most Holy Place because of the blood of Jesus. By his death, Jesus opened a new and life-giving way through the curtain into the Most Holy Place.
Hebrews 10:19-20

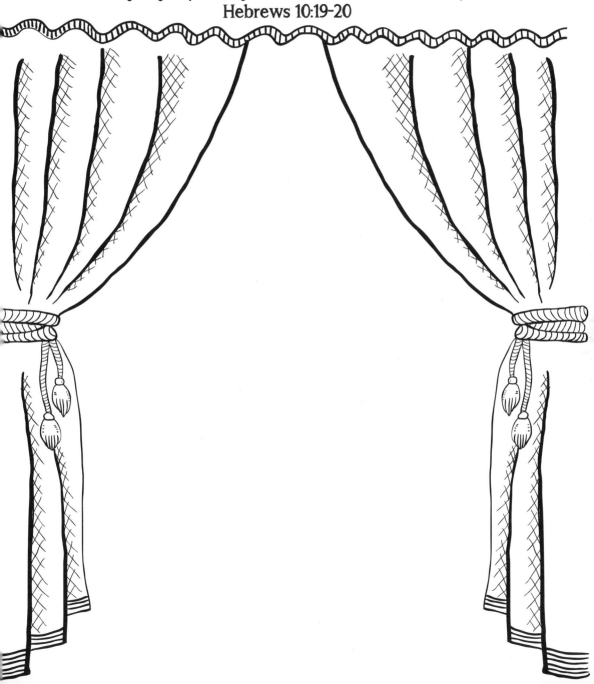

A Fiery Ordeal

READ: Daniel 3

THINK

As time went on, Israel continued to reject God, and eventually God judged their sin by allowing them to be conquered by Babylon. God's people were carried away from their homeland, once again slaves to a more powerful nation. But there were some who remained faithful to God, including Shadrach, Meshach, and Abednego. These young Israelite men loved God so much that they refused to bow down to the king's statue—even though their disobedience meant that they would be cast into a fiery furnace. They knew that bowing down to anyone other than God is wrong because we are to worship the Lord and serve only Him. They trusted that God could save them from the fiery furnace, but even if He didn't, they still did not want to bow down to the king's statue because they loved God.

As you might expect, the king was angry at their disobedience. He made the furnace so hot that it killed the men who had to throw Shadrach, Meshach, and Abednego into it. But when the king looked in later, he saw that not only were the three Israelite men walking around unharmed in the fire, there was also a fourth man who looked like an angel with them. God had saved Shadrach, Meshach, and Abednego, and they came out of the furnace not even smelling like smoke! Not one hair on their heads was burned. God is that powerful.

DRAW:

In the furnace on the next page, draw Daniel's three friends and the mysterious figure who joined them. Thank God for His power to rescue His people from danger.

If we are thrown into the blazing furnace, the God whom we serve is able to save us. He will rescue us from your power, Your Majesty.

Daniel 3:17

For Such a Time

READ: Esther 4:10-17; 7:1-10

THINK

The book of Esther tells about another time when God's people were being persecuted. An evil advisor to the Persian king hatched a plot to have all the Jews killed. But God had placed one Jewish woman, Esther, in the king's court as his wife. Esther's uncle Mordecai told her about the danger her people were in and begged her to speak to the king. It was a dangerous thing he was asking her to do, because even asking to speak to the king could get a person killed. But Esther believed that God had put her in that position to save His people. And so with some encouragement from her uncle and the prayers of God's people supporting her, Esther bravely approached the king, revealed her nationality, and asked the king to spare the Jews.

Not only did the king spare them—he also had his evil advisor killed in the same way he had plotted for the Jews to be killed. God had saved His people, and He had done it through the courage of one young Jewish woman. God can use you, too. Maybe there is a problem you see that God has put you in a position to solve. If He has laid something on your heart and enabled you to do something about it, take courage like Esther did, ask people to pray for you, and then do what God is calling you to do.

DRAW:

What are some big problems you see in your school, in your town, or in the world that you would like to help solve? Draw pictures to represent those issues that are on your heart, and then ask God to show you what He wants YOU to do about them.

Who knows if perhaps you were made queen for just such a time as this?

Esther 4:14

Rebuilding Jerusalem

THINK

READ: Nehemiah 1:1–2:8

God's people were conquered and taken from the land God had promised them, but God didn't forget about them. In time, He caused the Persian king Cyrus to allow them to go back to their homeland and begin rebuilding the Temple under the direction of a man named Ezra. About 100 years later, there was once again a Temple in Jerusalem, but the city was vulnerable to attack because there was no city wall. On top of that, they didn't have strong leadership. God placed these problems on the heart of Nehemiah, the Jewish man who served as cupbearer to the new king of Persia, Artaxerxes. Nehemiah prayed that God would remember His promises and rescue His people. And then Nehemiah went to the king and told him about the problem. He asked the king to allow him to go to Jerusalem and rebuild the city wall.

God gave Nehemiah favor with the king, and he was allowed to lead the people in rebuilding the wall. Like Esther, God put the right person in the right place to solve a big problem. It wasn't easy, but Nehemiah was courageous and strong to do God's work even when it was hard. God is faithful to keep His promises, and He enables us to be part of His work.

DRAW:

Do you ever have to stick with a job when you'd rather quit?
On the next page, draw a picture of something you have to stick with, and then thank God that He's using your hard work to make a difference.

On October 2 the wall was finished—
just fifty-two days after we had begun.
When our enemies and the surrounding nations
heard about it, they were frightened and humiliated.
They realized this work had been done with the help of our God.

Nehemiah 6:15-16

Silence

READ: Psalm 119:33-40

THINK

Have you ever sat in absolute silence, just you and your thoughts? Try it right now: set a timer for three minutes and go someplace quiet. If you're not used to it, even a couple minutes of silence can seem to stretch on forever. Now try to imagine 400 years of silence. It sounds like torture, doesn't it? Well that's what God's people faced in the time between the last prophet from the Old Testament and the coming of Jesus in the New Testament. They had the promises God made to Adam, Abraham, Isaac, and Jacob that He would one day send a rescuer—someone to save them. But it seemed like maybe God had forgotten. Not one word from God for 400 years. But God never forgets, and He never stops faithfully loving us. During those 400 years He was working His plan, in His time, just like He always does. Jesus was coming, and through Him everyone who believes can be saved from sin and have eternal life.

We don't have to worry about God being silent anymore because we have all of His words to us in the Bible, and we also have the Holy Spirit living in our hearts. He speaks to us by making God's words in the Bible come alive to us. God is speaking; are you listening?

DRAW:

Anytime we want to hear from God, all we have to do is read the Bible. What a gift that is! Do you fully appreciate it and take advantage of it? Color the next page and memorize the verse. Then thank God for speaking through the Bible and the Holy Spirit.

ALL SCRIPTURE IS INSPIRED BY GOD

& is useful to teach us what is **TRUE** and make us realize what is wrong in our lives.

IT CORRECTS US when we are wrong and **TEACHES US TO DO WHAT IS RIGHT.**

GOD USES IT TO PREPARE & EQUIP his people to do every **GOOD WORK.**

2 Timothy 3:16-17

THE NEW
TESTAMENT

A Willing Servant

READ: Luke 1:26-38

THINK

God was about to speak, and the message would be very loud and very clear. You see, He was going to come Himself, God in human flesh, to fulfill the promise He made way back in the Garden of Eden. Jesus was coming to save the world. You might think He would do it with royal fanfare. After all, He is the King of everything. But instead He chose to do it by coming as a tiny, helpless baby—born to a young and inexperienced mother named Mary. God uses weak people to show His strength. The angel Gabriel appeared to Mary, who was probably about 13 years old at the time, and told her that she would have a baby, and He would be the Son of God, the Messiah, the One who had been promised when sin first entered the world. The Savior was coming in the most surprising way.

I bet Mary was afraid when the angel came, and even more afraid to hear she was going to have a baby even before she was married, but she responded with full trust in God. She said, "I am the Lord's servant." In other words, whatever You ask me to do, God, I will do it. Even if it is a big job and I'm scared. I will trust You to help me.

DRAW:

Do you ever feel small and weak, like God can't possibly use you to do big things? Take it from Mary: if you trust God and are willing to obey Him, He can and will use you. On the next page, draw a picture of what you think the angel looked like. Think about how you will respond the next time God asks you to do something scary.

Mary responded, "I am the Lord's servant.
May everything you have said about me come
true." And then the angel left her.

Luke 1:38

Promise Fulfilled

READ: Luke 2:1-20

THINK

You probably know quite a bit about the birth of Jesus. You've seen pictures of Mary and Joseph's journey to Bethlehem, the inn that was totally full, and Jesus' birth in a stable, surrounded by farm animals. You know about how the angels appeared to the shepherds, who then went to worship Jesus, and how the star guided the wise men to Him as well. But did you ever think about what it all means?

Even in the circumstances of Jesus' birth, which I think we all agree were quite remarkable, we see an important truth about Him. Here it is: Jesus came for all of us. The shepherds and the wise men, the rich and the poor, the respected and the people no one thought were worth much. He came for you and for me and for everyone else on the earth. And He did it because He had made a promise to love us with a forever love, and to free us from the grip sin has on our hearts. I hope today you will take some time to praise God for the gift of Jesus. Join with the angels, with the shepherds, with the wise men, and with Mary and Joseph. Let everything that has breath praise the Lord, for He is worthy of all our worship. He kept His promise and came to save us!

DRAW:

On the next page, draw yourself worshiping
God with the angels of heaven.

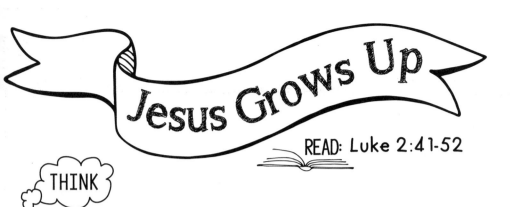

Jesus Grows Up

READ: Luke 2:41-52

THINK

We don't know a lot about Jesus' growing-up years. We do know that He lived the normal life of a Jewish boy during that period in history. He had annoying little brothers and sisters. He had to obey His parents even though sometimes there was something more interesting to do than the chores they needed Him to do. And He celebrated all the religious festivals required by Jewish law, including a yearly pilgrimage to the Temple for Passover.

One year when they were at the Temple Jesus lost track of time. Several days later His frantic parents found Him sitting at the feet of the Jewish rabbis, learning about the Jewish law. But He wasn't just learning, He was also teaching. Everyone who heard Jesus knew that He had a special authority, though they didn't realize that His authority came from the fact that He is God. Now, if Jesus sat at the Temple learning and teaching—and then returned to His parents and obeyed them, then we should as well. It's important to work at growing in wisdom as well as in stature. We should study the Bible so we can learn everything we can about God's love and how He wants us to live.

DRAW:

You're growing on the outside—but are you growing on the inside, in the ways that really matter? Are you growing in wisdom and in favor with God and with all the people, just like Jesus did? Draw some of the things that help you grow on the outside and the inside, and then thank God for giving you all these tools to help you grow wise and strong in Jesus.

Jesus grew in wisdom and in stature
and in favor with God and all the people.
Luke 2:52

The Temptation of Christ

READ: Luke 4:1-13

THINK

In addition to living the life of a normal Jewish boy at that time in history, Jesus also experienced sadness and temptation, just like us. Hebrews 4:15 says, "He faced all of the same testings we do, yet he did not sin."

Right at the beginning of His ministry, Jesus was led by the Holy Spirit into the wilderness, where He did not have anything to eat or drink for 40 days. I don't know about you, but if I go even 6 hours without anything to eat or drink, I get pretty cranky! Satan took advantage of the situation and told Jesus to turn stones into bread. Jesus could have done that, easily, but God wanted Him to rely on His strength alone. And so Jesus said no. Next Satan tempted Him to gain the glory of the world by worshiping Satan—something that was obviously wrong. Again Jesus refused. Finally Satan told Him to throw Himself off the Temple and have the angels protect Him. Again Jesus said no, because doing this would test God's faithfulness. Each time He said no to Satan, Jesus quoted a verse from the Bible, because the Bible is what tells us right from wrong. When we are tempted, we should follow Jesus' example and use Scripture to know what is right and have the courage to do it.

DRAW:

What are some wrong things that you are sometimes tempted to do? How do you fight against these temptations? Draw some of the ways you can fight against temptation—starting with the Bible.

The temptations in your life are no different from what others experience.

AND GOD IS FAITHFUL.

He will not allow the temptation to be more than you can stand. When you are tempted, he will

SHOW YOU A WAY OUT

so that YOU CAN ENDURE.

1 Corinthians 10:13

The Baptism of Jesus

READ: Matthew 3:13-17

THINK

Have you been baptized? Some Christians baptize their children as infants, believing that baptism is a sign that the child is part of God's covenant promises and showing that they hope that when the child grows up, he or she will decide to follow Jesus. Others are baptized as adults to show that they have already made the decision to die to their sins and live for Jesus. Either way, it's an important symbol that represents the fact that the only way we can be cleansed of our sins is by repenting and believing in Jesus. Through baptism, we are symbolically buried with Jesus in death and raised to new life in Him.

So then why was Jesus baptized? Right at the beginning of His ministry He went to His cousin, John, who was baptizing people, and asked him to baptize Him. Since Jesus never sinned, He didn't need to be saved from anything. So for Him, baptism was a symbolic representation of what He had come to earth to do: His death, burial, and resurrection. It was a proclamation that Jesus was the promised Messiah who would save His people from their sins. That is why after He was baptized, the Spirit descended on Him in the form of a dove and the Father spoke from heaven, saying, "This is My dearly loved Son, who brings Me great joy."

DRAW:

Draw a dove descending on Jesus. Thank God for the new life that Jesus brought when He died on the cross, was raised from the dead, and ascended to glory.

After his baptism, as Jesus came up out of the water, the heavens were opened and he saw the Spirit of God descending like a dove and settling on him. And a voice from heaven said, "This is my dearly loved Son, who brings me great joy."

Matthew 3:16-17

Jesus Calls the Disciples

READ: Luke 5:1-11

THINK

During His ministry on earth, Jesus had an inner circle of helpers called the disciples. These men traveled with Him for three years, learning from Him, watching what He did, and helping Him. Four of them, Simon Peter, Andrew, James, and John, started out as fishermen on the Sea of Galilee. One day the crowds were so huge that Jesus decided to teach from a boat, and the boats that happened to be there were the ones belonging to these four men.

When He was done teaching, Jesus told Simon Peter to push off into deeper water and put his fishing nets back into the water. Now, Jesus was a carpenter, not a fisherman. These four men who fished for a living knew that 1) the best time to catch fish is at night and 2) they had not caught any fish at all the previous night. What Jesus was asking them to do was crazy. Nevertheless, Simon said, "Because you say so, I will" and obeyed. And you know what? There were so many fish he had to call his friends over to help haul in the catch. They caught so many fish that both boats were on the verge of sinking. It was a miracle, and seeing it made all four men decide to follow Jesus.

DRAW:

Jesus is asking each of us to say to Him, "Because You say so, I will." When we choose to obey Him like that, no questions asked, Jesus gives us a greater purpose to live for: joining in His mission to save people from their sins by telling them about Him. What is God asking you to do today? On the next page, draw a picture of one way you can obey God today.

"Master," Simon replied, "we worked hard all last night and didn't catch a thing. But if you say so, I'll let the nets down again." And this time their nets were so full of fish they began to tear!

Luke 5:5-6

Jesus the Healer

READ: Mark 2:1-12

THINK

One of the things Jesus did during His time on earth was heal people. That really got people's attention and drew crowds! Mark 2 describes a time when Jesus was teaching in someone's house, and it was so crowded that the doorway was blocked. But some men had brought their paralyzed friend to be healed, and they wouldn't give up. So they opened up a hole in the roof and lowered the paralyzed man down on his mat. Jesus was impressed by their faith in Him and their devotion to their friend, but rather than declaring the man healed, He said, "My child, your sins are forgiven."

How do you think you would have reacted to Jesus' words? Would you have been disappointed? Surprised? Some of the people listening were shocked and dismayed. How dare Jesus declare the man forgiven—only God can do that! Well, of course we know that Jesus could declare him forgiven because He *is* God. And Jesus knew that the man's greatest need wasn't physical healing, which only lasts through this life, but spiritual healing—the forgiveness of sins, which lasts now and through eternity. Jesus can heal our bodies when they are sick, but the bigger need each one of us has is to be forgiven. To have our relationship with God restored and be able to spend forever with Jesus after we die.

DRAW:

Have you asked Jesus to forgive your sins? Do you spend more time asking Him to give you a happy life or asking Him to help you live for Him? As you color in the picture of Jesus healing the man, ask Jesus to take care of your physical needs *and* your spiritual needs.

"I will prove to you that the Son of Man has the authority on earth to forgive sins."

Mark 2:10

Jesus Calms the Storm

READ: Mark 4:35-41

THINK

It had been a long day. The crowds were everywhere, and Jesus and the disciples were tired. So they got in their boat to go to the other side of the lake. Jesus went to the back of the boat to take a little nap. Suddenly a huge storm came up. It was so wild and terrifying that the disciples were sure the boat was about to break apart and they would all drown. Yet still Jesus slept. Did He not care that they were about to die?

Finally the disciples woke Jesus up, and He simply said, "Silence! Be still!" and instantly the sea was calm. Not a wave or ripple in sight. No more howling wind, just absolute calm. It was so sudden that the stillness was even more terrifying than the storm—*who was this man, that even the wind and waves obeyed Him?*

Jesus saw their fear, and He asked, "Why are you afraid?" We should ask that same question of ourselves. What is there to be afraid of? Jesus loves us and will take care of us, and He is far more powerful than anything life can throw at us.

DRAW:

Do you have anything in your life that feels like a big, scary storm? Draw or write those things in the water around the boat. Then write JESUS CALMS THE STORM on the boat. Remember that no matter what you face in life, Jesus is bigger and more powerful, and He can bring peace to any situation.

When Jesus woke up, he rebuked the wind and said to the waves, "Silence! Be still!" Suddenly the wind stopped, and there was a great calm.

Mark 4:39

Jesus Teaches Us to Pray

READ: Matthew 6:5-15

THINK

How often do you pray? Prayer is just talking to God, and you can do that anytime and anywhere because God is always listening. That's pretty incredible, isn't it? The mighty Creator, your loving heavenly Father, wants to hear all your thoughts and feelings and requests. You can pray when you're in trouble, when you're happy, and when you're sad. But sometimes it's hard to know what to pray about. Fortunately, Jesus taught us how to pray in the Bible. Here is what He said, in a nutshell:

Pray with a sincere heart, being honest before God. Go ahead and say what you're really thinking and feeling, because He knows it already! Use this pattern:

Dear Father, make Your name holy. Bring Your Kingdom to earth so that more and more people worship and serve You. May everything be done according to what You want, just like it is in heaven. Here is what I need today—will You provide it? Forgive me for all the things I do wrong, and help me to forgive those who hurt me. Help me to do what is right, and keep me from harm. Amen.

 DRAW:

Now it's your turn.
On the next page, draw or
write your prayer to Jesus. Tell Him how you're feeling,
what you're worried about, and what you hope for. Don't forget
to thank Him for all the good things He has done for you!

Your Father knows exactly what you need even before you ask him! Matthew 6:8

Living Water

READ: John 4:1-30

THINK

One day Jesus was traveling through a place called Samaria during the hottest part of the day. Now, Jews didn't like Samaritans, so even walking through that area was dangerous. But there He was, sitting by Himself at a well, sweaty, tired, and thirsty. Along came a Samaritan woman. Most women would get water in the early morning hours, when it was cooler, but this woman didn't like to do that because the other women laughed at her and looked down on her. She had done a lot of bad things in her life, and she didn't have many friends.

Jesus saw this lonely woman and cared about her. So He asked her to give Him a drink. She was surprised, since He was a Jew and a man—two good reasons for Him not to talk to her. Then Jesus told her that if she knew who He was and what He could offer her, she would ask Him for living water. As they kept talking, Jesus told her all about herself—secret things she didn't tell anyone else. In that moment, she knew that Jesus was God's Son, the promised Messiah, and she knew that she wanted Him to save her.

DRAW:

Jesus offers living water that lasts forever. That doesn't mean we won't ever need a drink of regular water. Living water is deep refreshment and joy in our souls. It is having life and happiness even on sad days. It is being able to love others even when they have hurt us. Have you asked Jesus for this kind of life inside you? On the next page, draw pictures of what Jesus' living water means to you.

"Those who drink the
water I give will never
be thirsty again.
It becomes a fresh,
bubbling spring within
them, giving them
eternal life."
John 4:14

The Bread of Life

READ: John 6:1-15

THINK

When was the last time you were really, really hungry? Maybe you were traveling, and you couldn't find a McDonald's for miles and miles. Or maybe you were at soccer practice and couldn't wait for it to end so you could have a snack. One day Jesus was teaching, and a huge crowd of about 10,000 people had gathered to listen. The only problem was that it was getting late, and no one had thought to bring food along. The people were hungry. Jesus told His disciples to feed the people, and they said, "All we have is one boy's lunch—five loaves and a few fish—and there is nothing for miles around. We can't fix this problem!"

So Jesus fed them. Miraculously, the boy's lunch held out and everyone ate all they wanted and there were still 12 baskets full of leftovers. Jesus had solved an immediate need—the people were hungry! But He was also showing that He is powerful enough to satisfy all our needs. He said, "I am the bread of life. Whoever comes to me will never be hungry again." In other words, if you're feeling empty inside, go to Jesus. If you're noticing that even the most wonderful things in life don't truly satisfy you, go to Jesus. When we spend our lives worshiping and serving and loving Him, we will find that we are truly happy in the deepest part of our souls.

DRAW:

On the next page, draw your favorite meal. Think about the true satisfaction that Jesus gives, which is more wonderful than the most delicious food we will ever eat.

Jesus replied, "I am the bread of life. Whoever comes to me will never be hungry again. Whoever believes in me will never be thirsty."

John 6:35

The Good Shepherd

READ: John 10:1-16

In Jesus' day, being a shepherd was a common profession. Shepherds lived with their flock of sheep and took care of them. When one ran away and got lost, the shepherd would search high and low until he found the sheep, and if it was injured he would put medicine and bandages on its wounds. Whenever the shepherd called, the sheep would come running at the sound of his voice. During the day, the shepherd would lead the sheep to the best grass and find fresh water for them to drink. At night, the shepherd would lead the sheep back to the sheepfold and sleep in front of the door so the sheep couldn't get out and predators couldn't get in.

That is a picture of how Jesus cares for His people. Everything that a good shepherd would do for his sheep, Jesus does for us. He leads us, provides for us, protects us, and heals us. Most of all, He loves us. Jesus is the best shepherd of all, and He sacrificed everything, giving up His life so that we can be with Him forever. Do you love Jesus the Good Shepherd, and do you listen for His voice so He can lead you to cool, clear streams of living water?

If you trust in Jesus, you are His precious lamb. On the next page, draw or write all the ways the Good Shepherd takes care of His sheep—which is how Jesus takes care of you! For instance, you might draw some bandages and write "Jesus heals me" or write next to the sheep's ear "Jesus helps me hear His voice."

"I am the good shepherd. The good shepherd sacrifices his life for his sheep."

John 10:11

Who Is My Neighbor?

READ: Luke 10:29-37

THINK

One day a religious teacher asked Jesus how he could have eternal life. Jesus reminded him of the law of Moses, which said that you must love the Lord with all your heart, soul, mind, and strength and love your neighbor as yourself. Not satisfied with that, the man followed up by asking Jesus who his neighbor was. He hoped Jesus would tell him that he only needed to love his friends.

Jesus answered by telling a story: there was a man who was attacked by robbers. They beat him, took everything he had, and left him half dead beside the road. Three different men came upon the scene and had three different reactions. The first one, a priest, crossed to the other side of the road so he wouldn't have to get too close to the injured man. The next man, a Temple worker, went over to see the man's predicament but didn't do anything to help. Finally, the third man, a racial enemy of the injured man, came onto the scene. He was the one Jesus' audience knew for sure wouldn't stop to help—yet he felt compassion, went over to the injured man, bandaged his wounds, and took him to a nearby inn and paid money for them to help him until he was healed. That man was the neighbor.

DRAW:

It's hard for us to understand just how surprising this story would have been to Jesus' listeners. The one they were sure was the villain of the story turned out to be the only one who showed mercy, while the religious people clearly did not obey God's law. Who are the people God has put in your life to show love to? Draw pictures of some of the people and situations where God wants you to love your neighbor as yourself.

"You must love the LORD your God with all your heart, all your soul, all your strength, and all your mind." And, "Love your neighbor as yourself."

Luke 10:27

Two Sisters

READ: Luke 10:38-42

Jesus often traveled, staying wherever He had been teaching that day. But He did have some friends in a town called Bethany whom He visited with often—a man named Lazarus and his sisters, Mary and Martha. One time when Jesus visited them, Mary spent His whole visit sitting at His feet, just listening to Jesus' teaching. She loved hearing about God and His Kingdom, and she loved being near to Jesus.

Meanwhile, Martha was very busy. She was fixing food, setting the table—and getting more and more angry. She grumbled as she worked: *Why isn't Mary helping me? I'd like to be sitting around listening to Jesus too, but someone has to get dinner on the table! It isn't fair!* Finally Martha couldn't stand it anymore, and she asked Jesus to tell Mary to help her. But Jesus just said, "You are worried and upset about things that don't matter. Mary has made a good choice."

I don't know what Martha did next—the Bible doesn't say—but I'd like to think that she sat next to Mary at Jesus' feet and served a simple meal. Do you ever get jealous, feeling like things aren't fair and you are doing all the work? Take a lesson from Martha. Don't get worried and upset over the details. Instead, sit at Jesus' feet and learn what He wants you to do.

{ DRAW: }

On the table, draw the table setting and food you would serve if Jesus came to your house. Think about the joy of just being near to Him, and thank God that you can be near to Him anytime you want, just by talking to Him.

The Lord said to her, "My dear Martha, you are worried and upset over all these details! There is only one thing worth being concerned about. Mary has discovered it, and it will not be taken away from her."

Luke 10:41-42

The Lost Son

READ: Luke 15:11-32

Sometimes it's hard for us to understand just how much God loves us. One day Jesus told a story to illustrate it. A younger son told his father, "I hate living here! I wish I could have my share of your money and go live somewhere else!" And so his father gave this ungrateful son his inheritance, and the son went away and spent all his money on wild parties. Eventually he ran out of money and found himself homeless, friendless, and working in the stinkiest job: feeding pigs. He was so desperate he even wished he could eat what the pigs were eating. He was out of options, and so he returned to his father hoping that maybe he could get a job as a servant in his father's house.

Meanwhile, the father missed his son. Each day he would sit on the porch and look down the road, hoping that he would see his son coming home. And then one glorious day he did! The father ran down the road, wrapped his arms around his son, put his robe on him, and welcomed him home. He was so overjoyed he threw a huge party for his lost son. He didn't care about how his son had rejected him or all the terrible things he had done, he was just happy to have his beloved son back home.

 DRAW:

Jesus told this story to illustrate how much God loves us. There is great rejoicing in heaven when someone decides to follow Jesus—no matter what terrible things that person has done. Have you experienced the love of God? As you color this picture, imagine yourself being hugged by God Himself.

In the same way, there is joy in the presence
of God's angels when even one sinner repents.

Luke 15:10

The Parable of the Farmer and His Seeds

READ: Matthew 13:1-23

THINK

Jesus taught a lot of people during His life on earth, and He teaches a lot of people today through His Word. But not everyone accepts and believes what He says. Jesus told a story to show the ways different people respond to the message of salvation through faith in Him.

A farmer went to sow seeds in his field. Some of it landed on the path, and birds came and ate it up. This represents the people whose hearts are too hard to understand Jesus' offer of salvation. Other seeds fell on shallow soil. The plants grew up quickly, but they had no roots, so they died. This represents people who hear about Jesus, receive Him with joy, but then fall away as soon as something bad happens to them. Some of the farmer's seeds fell among thorns, and the life was choked out of them before they had a chance to grow. This seed represents people who hear the message of Jesus and maybe want to believe it, but they are too busy worrying about life and earning money to focus on the gospel, so there is no fruit in their lives. Fortunately, some of the farmer's seeds fell on good soil, grew into healthy plants, and produced fruit. This represents people who hear and understand God's Word and help others to understand and believe it as well.

DRAW:

What kind of heart do you have? Do you receive God's Word with joy and tell others about Jesus? On the next page, draw the four kinds of soil and what happens to the seeds on that kind of soil.

The seed that fell on good soil represents those who truly hear and understand God's word and produce a harvest of thirty, sixty, or even a hundred times as much as had been planted!

Matthew 13:23

Jesus Walks on Water

READ: Matthew 14:22-33

THINK

✿ Jesus often went off by Himself to pray. One night He did that and told the disciples to get back in the boat and cross to the other side of the lake. Now, the Sea of Galilee was known for having storms suddenly come up with no warning. Remember the time Jesus was asleep in the boat during a storm? I bet the disciples remembered it too! Nevertheless, Jesus insisted and they obeyed.

Sure enough, a strong wind came up and the disciples struggled to keep the boat from sinking. But more terrifying than the storm was what they saw at about three o'clock in the morning: Jesus was walking toward them—just walking right on top of the water as if He was walking through a field on a beautiful, calm day. At first they wondered if it was a ghost, but then He talked to them. Peter said, "If it's really You, Jesus, tell me to walk on the water to meet You." Jesus told him to come, so Peter hopped out of the boat and walked on the water too. Then he noticed the big waves and the strong wind, and he started to sink. "Help me, Lord!" he cried out. Jesus reached out and pulled Peter back up. "Why did you doubt Me?" Jesus asked.

DRAW:

Whenever you are afraid or overwhelmed, you can reach out to Jesus and say, "Help me, Lord!" and Jesus will reach down to help you. As you color in the picture on the next page, imagine that you are Peter, sinking in the waves, and that Jesus is reaching out His hand to pull you up.

Jesus immediately reached out and grabbed him.
"You have so little faith," Jesus said.
"Why did you doubt me?"

Matthew 14:31

Little Children Come to Jesus

READ: Matthew 19:13-15

Have you ever heard someone say, "bless you!" Maybe someone has said it to you after you sneeze. That's a funny custom. In the time of the Bible, blessing was an important part of the way parents cared for their children. Parents spoke words of hope and happiness over their children, and that was called blessing.

When Jesus was teaching and performing miracles, some parents wanted Him to speak a special word of blessing for their children. So they brought their children to where He was teaching and tried to push their children to the front of the crowd so He would pray for them. Now, in those days children weren't considered very important, so Jesus' disciples tried to shoo them away. They thought Jesus had more important things to do. Imagine their surprise when Jesus said, "No, let them come to Me. Don't stop them!" He drew the children close, and He said, "The Kingdom of Heaven belongs to those who are like these children." Then Jesus blessed them. He cared for the little ones whom no one else thought were important, and He showed it by putting them on His lap and telling them He loved them and wanted good things for them.

DRAW:

Wouldn't it be nice to get a hug from Jesus and hear Him say He loves you? You can't see Him in person, but when you pray, it's like you're climbing onto Jesus' lap and talking to Him like a friend. Color the picture of Jesus on the next page, and draw yourself in the picture, being blessed by Jesus.

Jesus said, "Let the children come to me. Don't stop them! For the Kingdom of Heaven belongs to those who are like these children."

Matthew 19:14

The Vine and the Branches

READ: John 15:1-17

THINK

Have you ever seen grape vines? They grow tall and strong and give us sweet grapes, delicious juice, and grape jelly. But if farmers just let the vines grow wild, they don't produce as much fruit. Farmers cut off branches that aren't growing well so that the nutrients from the plant can be used to grow the biggest and best grapes.

Jesus said that our relationship with Him should be like that. He is the vine. That means He is the one who has all the life. We are like the branches, and if we just stay attached to Him, we will have His life in us. As long as we are attached to Jesus, we will bear fruit—spiritual fruit. We will become more and more loving, joyful, peaceful, patient, kind, good, faithful, gentle, and self-controlled. Our only job is to stay close to Jesus. We do that by reading the Bible every day, praying, and going to church to learn more about Him. Sometimes Jesus will have to take something out of our lives that has become more important to us than Him, or that is going to cause us harm, but if we just continue to stay close to Jesus, we will be joyful even during that process.

DRAW:

On the vine on the next page, draw flowers and fruit. Ask God to help you stay close to Him so you can bear the fruit He wants: love and joy and peace through the power of the Holy Spirit working in you.

"Yes, I am the vine; you are the branches.
Those who remain in me, and I in them,
will produce much fruit. For apart
from me you can do nothing."
John 15:5

Jesus Rides into Jerusalem

READ: Mark 11:1-11

THINK

Remember the promise we talked about way back in the Garden of Eden, when God said He would send someone to defeat Satan and save us from sin and death? Now we know that person was Jesus. By this point His followers thought that Jesus was the Savior, but they didn't know how He was going to save them. They expected Him to become king of Israel and rule over the nation. After all, that is what kings do. So when they heard that Jesus was headed for Jerusalem, they did the only thing they knew to do—they got ready to welcome the conquering king.

It was a little surprising that instead of a fancy horse, Jesus was riding on a donkey, but never mind that. As Jesus rode into town, the people spread their coats on the ground and waved palm branches. That was how they welcomed kings, and Jesus was the King. They shouted, "Hosanna! Blessed is the one who comes in the name of the Lord!"

Jesus deserved their praises, just as He deserves our praises. But the fact that He was riding on a donkey should have tipped them off that this was a humble king, and the kingdom He was bringing was in people's hearts, not in city hall. Just one week after this triumphal entry, the same crowds shouted for Jesus' crucifixion, and they sentenced the King of kings to die a criminal's death.

DRAW:

Are you like the crowds in this story? Do you welcome Jesus and praise Him one moment, then betray Him and sin against Him the next? Draw yourself in the picture of the crowd on the next page, and decide in your heart to be someone who lives for Jesus.

Jesus was in the center of the procession, and the people all around him were shouting, "Praise God! Blessings on the one who comes in the name of the LORD! Blessings on the coming Kingdom of our ancestor David! Praise God in highest heaven!"

Mark 11:9-10

The Last Supper

READ: John 13:1-17

THINK

It was the night of the Passover, when all the Jews had a special meal to remember how God led His people out of slavery in Egypt. Jesus' disciples didn't know that Jesus was about to die to save them—to sacrifice Himself as the Lamb of God. They were just ready to celebrate the feast.

Imagine their surprise when Jesus—their leader and teacher—got up from the table, took off His robe, wrapped a towel around His waist, and began to wash their feet. He was acting like a lowly slave, taking on the very worst job of the household. Their feet were dirty and smelly from walking in the desert dust. Peter, the one who always seemed to have something to say, tried to make Jesus stop. He knew that he was not worthy of this expression of love. But Jesus insisted, and He told them that they should follow His example. If He, their master and teacher, would humble Himself to serve them in the most demeaning way possible, then how much more should they serve one another?

DRAW:

When was the last time you served someone without expecting anything in return? What could you do today to show love like Jesus did at the Last Supper? Draw a picture of what you plan to do—then do it!

"Since I, your Lord and Teacher, have washed your feet, you ought to wash each other's feet. I have given you an example to follow. Do as I have done to you."

John 13:14-15

The Moment That Changed Everything

 THINK

READ: Matthew 27:32-54

After the Last Supper, Jesus went to a quiet place to pray. He was very sad about what He knew He had to do next, but He told His Father that if He had to die, He was willing to do it. Then some soldiers came and arrested Him, and Jesus was put on trial. Imagine it—the King of the universe, who had lived an absolutely perfect life, on trial. The soldiers made fun of Him and spat on Him. The crowds shouted, "Crucify Him!" Even Jesus' disciples ran away from Him. Yet through it all, Jesus did not try to defend Himself. He knew it had to be this way.

Then they took Jesus to a hillside, nailed His hands and feet to a wooden cross, and hung Him up to die. Do you know why He did it? Jesus was taking the punishment for all our sins. All the wrong things you have done, and all the wrong things I have done, and all the wrong things that everyone in all of history has done, were placed on Jesus. Because He had never done anything wrong, Jesus could take the punishment we deserved so that we won't have to die for our own sins. It was the worst moment ever—God the Creator dying on a cross—but also the best moment ever because it meant that we can be forgiven! The curse of sin and death was broken, and Satan is defeated.

 DRAW:

As you color in the picture of the cross, imagine all the wrong things you do being put on Jesus. He took the punishment for your sins so you can live with Him forever! Thank Jesus for paying the price so you can be saved from your sins.

Christ suffered for our
sins once for all time. He never sinned,
but he died for sinners to bring you safely home to God.
He suffered physical death, but he was raised to life in the Spirit.
1 Peter 3:18

The Resurrection

THINK

Jesus' followers thought it was all over. They had thought Jesus was the Messiah, but then instead of taking control of the government in Jerusalem like a Messiah ought to do, He had been put on trial and hung. Now He was buried in a tomb. Everything they had worked for was gone, and on top of that their beloved teacher was dead, so they couldn't even ask Him what they should do next. They were very sad and discouraged.

Early on Sunday morning, as soon as they were allowed to do so, the women who loved Jesus went to honor His body by putting spices on it. Imagine their shock and terror when they found that the tomb was open and two angels stood outside it! And then the angel told them Jesus was alive! How could this have happened?

Because Jesus was the perfect Son of God, death couldn't hold Him back. He rose again from the dead. Jesus won, overturning the curse that had been made in the Garden of Eden after Adam and Eve sinned. Now we can be freed from the power of sin and spend eternity with Jesus in heaven, rather than dying an eternal death for our sins.

This is our hope!

DRAW:

Jesus was raised from the dead, and because He was raised from the dead we can be also. If you have told Jesus that you believe that He died to take the punishment for your sins, you will be raised with Him and live with Him forever. If you haven't already prayed to Jesus, telling Him that you are a sinner and that you believe He can forgive you, why don't you do so while you color in the picture of the empty tomb?

The women
were terrified and bowed with their
faces to the ground. Then the men asked, "Why
are you looking among the dead for someone
who is alive? He isn't here!
He is risen from the dead!"

Luke 24:5-6

The Next Chapter

READ: Matthew 28:16-20

THINK

☷ You may think the story of Jesus is over at this point. After all, Jesus died and was raised from the dead. That was what He came to do, and the job was finished. But the story continues, even today, and it includes you and me.

Jesus spent a few weeks on earth after the resurrection, but then it was time for Him to return to His glorious throne in heaven. So He gathered the disciples together on a mountaintop and gave them His final instructions. He said, "Go and tell everyone you meet about Me! Tell them that they can be saved from their sins and live for Me. Baptize them and teach them everything I have taught you about how to live." He also promised that He would be with them while they did this important (and sometimes scary) job.

These commands are for us, as well. If you believe in Jesus, you have an important job to do: tell others about Him so they can believe in Him too. Knowing that Jesus will forgive you and having the certainty that when you die, you will go to be with Him forever, is such wonderful good news that you should want to share it with everyone you meet. What a privilege it is to be part of the next chapter of Jesus' mission!

DRAW:

Have you told anyone about Jesus? Draw a picture of yourself telling someone about Him, and write the names of a few people who may not yet know Him. Then make a plan to share the good news with them!

"Therefore, go and make disciples of all the nations, baptizing them in the name of the Father and the Son and the Holy Spirit. Teach these new disciples to obey all the commands I have given you. And be sure of this: I am with you always, even to the end of the age."

Matthew 28:19-20

The Holy Spirit

READ: Acts 2:1-12, 32-33

THINK

Jesus had told His disciples that He would send a helper to them, but He hadn't said exactly what that meant. They were about to find out! After Jesus ascended into heaven, the believers weren't sure what to do next. They were afraid that they might be put on trial and sentenced to death as well, so they hid out and prayed. Suddenly, they heard a sound like roaring wind, and then flames of fire appeared and settled on each of them. After that, they could suddenly speak in languages they didn't know. What was going on?

Well, this was the helper Jesus had promised: the Holy Spirit. You see, there is one God, but He is made up of three separate persons. It's a little confusing, even for grown-ups, but the important thing to know is that the Holy Spirit is God who lives inside you. He helps you to know Jesus better and do what is right. When Jesus was on earth, He could only be in one place at a time because He is God in human skin, limited in the ways we are. After He returned to heaven, God the Holy Spirit could come and be everywhere all at the same time. That means that if you love Jesus, you have the Holy Spirit in you!

DRAW:

You may not have thought much about the Holy Spirit before, but it's important to know that if you believe in Jesus, God is with you every moment. When you are scared, you can turn to Him. When you are doing something hard, He is right there with you. Draw or write about some of the times when you need the Holy Spirit to help you.

"But when the Father sends the Advocate as my representative—that is, the Holy Spirit—he will teach you everything and will remind you of everything I have told you."

John 14:26

A Blinding Light

THINK

The Jewish religious leaders of the day didn't like Jesus' followers any better than they had liked Jesus Himself. They thought that crucifying Jesus would take care of the problem, but now His followers were making even more trouble. And so they set out to persecute and imprison anyone who followed Jesus. One of the worst persecutors was a man named Saul. He thought he was doing the right thing by stamping out Christianity, but of course he just didn't know the truth yet. Fortunately, that was about to change.

One day Saul was walking down the street, on the way to capture some Christians, when suddenly a bright light shone around him and blinded him. A voice from heaven said, "I am Jesus, the one you are persecuting!" Saul was speechless, as were the men who were with him, but he obeyed God's voice and went to Damascus. Three days later, God told a man named Ananias to go find Saul and tell him about Jesus. Now, Ananias knew that Saul hated Christians, and he told God he thought this was a bad idea, but in the end he obeyed God and went anyway. When Ananias prayed with him, Saul was filled with the Holy Spirit, believed in Jesus, was baptized, and immediately began preaching about Jesus. Talk about a turnaround!

DRAW:

When people believe in Jesus, their whole lives are changed. They have new priorities, new ways of thinking, and new ways of behaving. Is there someone you know who needs to hear about Jesus? Think about that question as you color the next page, and then go and tell whoever Jesus brings to mind how much God loves them.

ANYONE WHO BELONGS TO CHRIST has become a NEW PERSON. THE OLD LIFE IS GONE; A NEW LIFE HAS BEGUN!

2 Corinthians 5:17

A Miraculous Escape

READ: Acts 12:3-19

THINK

The persecution of Christians continued, and the apostle Peter was put in prison. All the followers of Jesus prayed that he would be released. The night before his trial, Peter was handcuffed to two soldiers, one on either side, to make sure he wouldn't escape. While he slept, suddenly there was a bright light and an angel of the Lord appeared before Peter. The angel woke him up, released him from his chains, and told him to get dressed and follow him. Peter obeyed, but he thought it was all a dream.

The angel led Peter out of the prison, past the gates of the city, and right to the house where all the believers had gathered to pray for him. At that point Peter realized it wasn't a dream after all, and he went and knocked on the door. The servant girl answered the door, saw that it was Peter, and was so surprised she ran back to where the people had gathered to pray without even opening the door. "Peter is standing at the door!" she said. No one believed her. But the knocking continued, so finally someone went to the door, and sure enough, there was Peter! God had freed him.

DRAW:

It's funny to think of Peter standing at the door, knocking and knocking, because no one believed that God would actually answer their prayers! But we often do that, too. What are you praying for that you will be surprised if God answers? Write or draw it on the door—and keep praying!

Keep on asking, and you will receive what you ask for. Keep on seeking, and you will find. Keep on knocking, and the door will be opened to you.

Matthew 7:7

Singing in Prison

THINK

Not too long after Peter's miraculous escape from prison, Paul and Silas found themselves in a similar predicament. They had made a lot of people angry by sending an evil spirit out of a slave girl. When the evil spirit was gone, the girl was a lot happier but the people who owned her had lost a lot of money. So Paul and Silas were beaten and thrown into jail.

I bet Paul and Silas were scared and discouraged as they sat chained in a prison cell, but do you know what they did? They sang praise songs. The Bible tells us to give thanks in all circumstances, and Paul and Silas certainly did that! Around midnight, there was an earthquake that made the doors of every prison cell open up. The jailer who was responsible for keeping everyone in prison was about to kill himself, since he was sure everyone had escaped, but Paul told him everyone was accounted for—no one had run away. Immediately the jailer decided he wanted to serve the God who had made Paul and Silas such good people, so he asked them how he could be saved. "Believe in the Lord Jesus and you will be saved," Paul told him. That's it. We can't do anything to earn our salvation. Jesus saves us when we put our trust in Him.

DRAW:

Becoming a Christian is pretty simple. Believe that Jesus died to save you from your sins, and you will be saved. Have you taken that step? If not, why don't you do it right now, while you color in the verse?

BELIEVE IN THE LORD JESUS & YOU WILL BE SAVED.

Acts 16:31

God's Armor

READ: Ephesians 6:10-18

THINK

While Paul was in prison, he wrote letters to churches, helping them learn more about Jesus and how God wanted them to live. In one of those letters, the one to the church in Ephesus, Paul told believers that we are in a spiritual battle against Satan and the powers of evil. In order to fight against Satan, God gives us special armor to put on each day. This armor consists of all the tools God gives us to help us stand firm in the truth of the gospel. Of course, these aren't literal pieces of armor—they are spiritual weapons to fight a spiritual battle.

God gives us the belt of truth and the body armor of God's righteousness. These things will protect our heart. He gives us shoes that help us be ready to spread the good news of how people can have peace with God. He gives us the shield of faith to extinguish Satan's arrows. For our head, He gives us the helmet of salvation. Our only offensive weapon is the sword of the Spirit, which is the Bible. The final instruction Paul gave is to pray all the time, in every situation. If we use the armor God gives us, we will be able to stand firm in the truth even when Satan attacks us.

DRAW:

On the figure on the next page, draw the pieces of armor God gives us to fight against Satan that are mentioned in this passage. For example, on the head, draw a helmet and write "helmet of salvation." Imagine yourself putting all these things on every day!

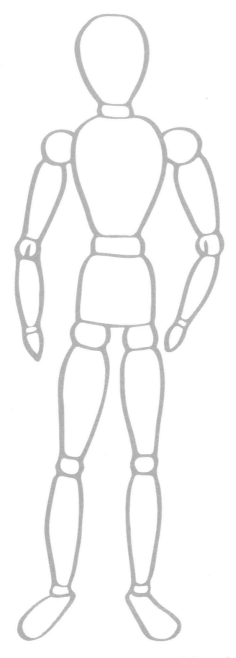

Put on all of God's armor so that you will be able to stand firm
against all strategies of the devil.
Ephesians 6:11

The Promise Fulfilled

READ: Revelation 21:1-7; 22:1-5

THINK

Do you remember the beginning of this book—and the beginning of the Bible—when God made a promise in the Garden of Eden to defeat sin and death? We saw how Jesus did that at the Cross. But you've probably noticed that the world isn't perfect yet. People still sin, and their bodies die. That's because we're still waiting for Jesus to finish the promise. One day He is going to return and establish a new heaven and a new earth where He will reign forever. He will give us new bodies that will live forever.

In the book of Revelation, God showed the apostle John what the new heaven and new earth will be like. This is the place where we will be with Jesus forever. It will be a beautiful place, full of light and precious gems. God will live there with us. He will wipe every tear from our eyes, and there will be no more death or sorrow or crying or pain. Everything will be new. In the middle of the city there will be a river of life, and anyone who is thirsty can drink from it freely. We will be completely, totally happy in Jesus. Doesn't that sound wonderful? This is the hope we live for!

DRAW:

On the next page, draw what you think heaven will look like. If you have some gold pens or crayons, you're going to need them!

God's home is now among his people!
He will live with them, and they will be his people.
God himself will be with them. He will wipe every tear
from their eyes, and there will be no more death or sorrow
or crying or pain. All these things are gone forever.

Revelation 21:3-4

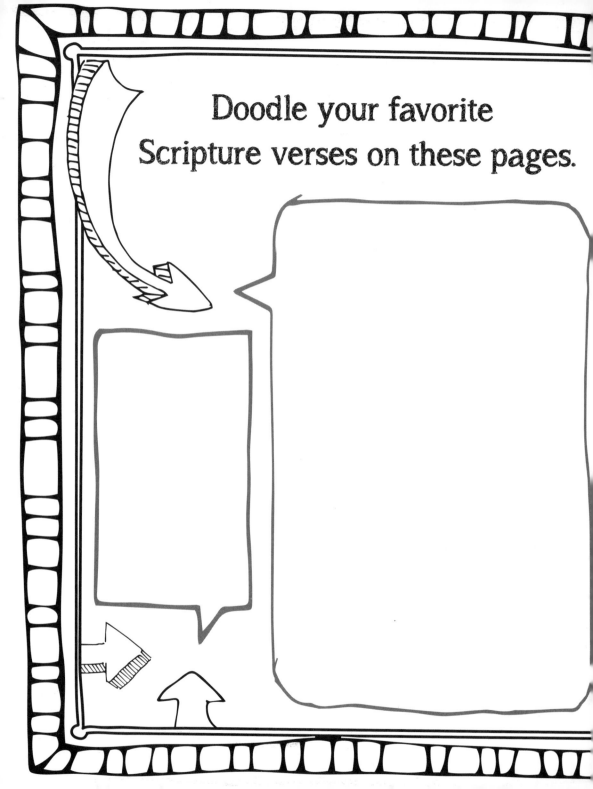

Doodle your favorite
Scripture verses on these pages.

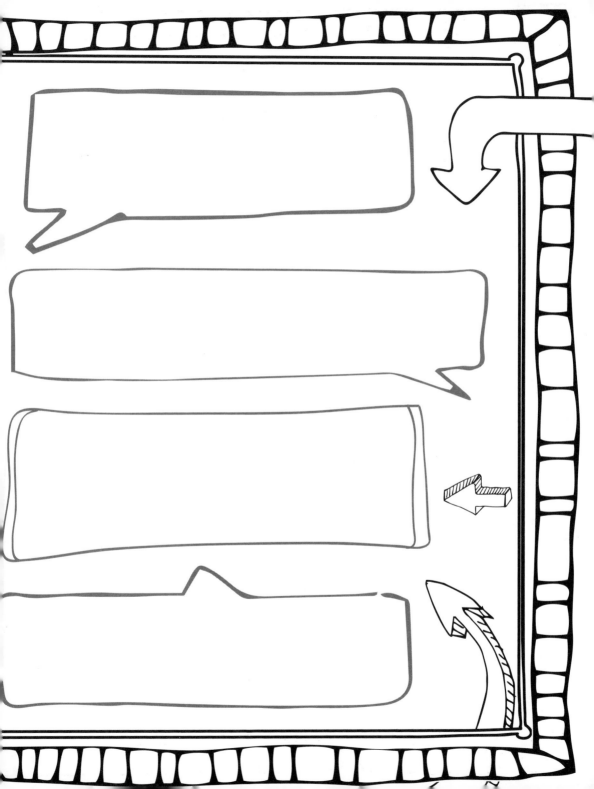

If you loved this book, check out
Doodle Devotions for Girls

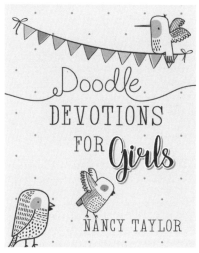

ISBN 978-1-4321-2711-4

Designed especially for preteen and teenage girls, this book is made to be doodled on. Every page in this 12-week devotional has an insight from God's Word and space for girls to respond — in whatever artistic way they choose.

Doodle Devotions for Girls offers practical ways to help girls think through and apply to their own lives what God says about salvation, body image, family issues, worship, dating, and more. The fun doodle prompts that accompany each devotion will also give them the boost they need to creatively express their faith.